from FELT to FABULOUS

Felt crafting may be the perfect creative activity! It's easy, fun for the entire family, and wonderfully inexpensive—and you can make things that are as practical as they are pretty. How about a Coffee Cup Cozy to keep your favorite beverage warm while your fingers stay cool? Or you can make a Hair Clip Holder to keep a girl's entire collection of hair clips together in one place. There's also a cute iPod/MP3 Cozy

Each pattern can be enlarged or reduced to the size you need for any project you want to make, whether it's a necklace pendant, ornament or stuffed toy. Once you get started, you'll probably think of dozens of additional ideas to create and share with family and friends!

meet KIMBERLY LAYTON

Kimberly Layton's creative adventure with felt had a truly sweet beginning—she made a cupcake brooch and fell in love with it! The tiny project was inspired by Japanese-style felt designs.

"That's why you see little faces on my fruit and cupcake patterns," Kimberly says. "My favorite projects are small animals, like the hedgehog. My son even has a pet hedgehog, so you know we're fans of the little creatures.

"I like dabbling in all kinds of crafts, but felt is my favorite. Some of these designs also look great with a mix of felt and designer fabric—try it!

"My other favorite pastime is traveling with my family. We've visited all the states in the lower 48 and have traveled with our children as far away as the Great Barrier Reef! Just mention the word 'go' and we are there!"

With plenty of adventure for her inspiration, Kimberly's creative life can't help but be sweet, indeed!

TABLE OF CONTENTS

To see Kimberly's latest patterns and a selection of designer wool felt and other crafting supplies, visit her online felt shop at KimberlyLayton.com. Kimberly also enjoys blogging and engaging with the community of artisans and Etsy sellers through her blog at EverythingEtsy.com. She can be found on Twitter (@EverythingEtsy) and Facebook (Facebook.com/EverythingEtsy).

LEISURE ARTS, INC.
Maumelle, Arkansas

Hair CLIPS, necklaces, & pins

Hair Clips are a fun and easy intro into crafting with felt. The small format requires very little investment in supplies and finishing is quick and easy. In addition to using them as hair accessories, you can thread a Hair Clip onto a chain or cord to make a necklace. Attach a pinback instead of a snap clip and your shape becomes a whimsical brooch.

Supplies
Not all designs require every supply listed.

- Felt scraps
- Embroidery floss
- Buttons
- Metal snap clips - 7/8" long for smaller hair clips and 1 1/2" long for larger hair clips
- Metal pinbacks - 3/4" long for pins
- Purchased chain/cord for necklaces

Any of the designs, pages 28-40, can be used to make any size hair clip, necklace, or pin simply by enlarging or reducing the patterns to the desired finished size. Ours range from 3/4" to 2 1/2" high.

*Please read **General Instructions**, pages 24-25, before beginning project. Follow **Using Patterns**, page 25, to adjust pattern size.*

Cutting
Cut 2 of each base shape and 1 of each embellishment shape from felt. **Note:** Only cut 1 base shape and 1 of each embellishment shape for the hedgehog, watermelon, turtle, and leaf.

Assembling
Many of the shapes can be assembled by simply referring to the photo. If more instruction is needed, follow **Clip Tips**, page 4, and **Embroidery Stitches**, page 26.

Use 3 strands of floss for embroidery details. When instructed to layer and sew bases together, use 6 strands and work a Running Stitch around the shape, approximately 1/8" from outer edges. **Note:** For very small hair clips, you may wish to use 3 strands for all stitching.

Refer to **Attaching The Snap Clip**, page 4, to sew a snap clip or pinback to the shape.

Instructions continued on page 4.

Mini Hair Clips
These cute little clips are just the right size for a small child's hair.

Sew a snap clip to 1 oval base. Embellish the remaining base with mini felt shapes, buttons, or embroidery. For the candy corn, cut 1 base shape and 1 each of the 3 candy corn shapes. Layer and sew bases together.

ATTACHING THE SNAP CLIP

Note: If making a pin, attach the pinback in the same manner as a snap clip.

Position snap clip on 1 side of the shape. You can make the hair clip face left or right so be sure to check the orientation. If you plan to use the shape on a necklace, position the snap clip vertically. Open snap clip. Using 6 strands of floss, follow **Figs. 1-2** to attach the snap clip to the shape.

Fig. 1

Fig. 2

CLIP TIPS *Instructions continued from page 2.*

Hedgehog *(Shown on page 3)*
Sew a snap clip to hedgehog base. Using Straight Stitches around the spikes and Running Stitches around the remaining edges, sew the fur to the hedgehog base. Attach the flower with a Cross Stitch and the nose with a Running Stitch. Work a Satin Stitch eye.

Owl *(Shown below)*
Sew a snap clip to 1 owl base. On remaining owl base, attach eyes with a Running Stitch. Work Satin Stitch pupils and beak. Backstitch feather details. Layer and sew bases together.

Bird *(Shown on page 3)*
Sew a snap clip to 1 bird base. On remaining bird base, attach wing with a Running Stitch. Work a Satin Stitch eye. Layer and sew bases together.

Dolphin *(Shown on page 3)*
Sew a snap clip to 1 dolphin base. On remaining dolphin base, work a Satin Stitch eye and Backstitch mouth. Layer and sew bases together.

Starfish *(Shown on page 29)*
Sew a snap clip to 1 starfish base. On remaining starfish base, work Satin Stitch eyes and a Backstitch mouth. Layer and sew bases together.

Goldfish *(Shown on page 3)*
Sew a snap clip to 1 goldfish base. On remaining goldfish base, work a Satin Stitch eye. Layer and sew bases together.

Strawberry *(Shown on page 3)*
Sew a snap clip to 1 strawberry base. On remaining strawberry base, work Satin Stitch eyes and a Backstitch mouth. Make Straight Stitch "seeds." Layer bases, insert leaf between layers and sew bases together.

Heart *(Shown on page 3)*
Sew a snap clip to 1 heart base. On remaining heart base, attach small heart with Running Stitches. Layer and sew bases together.

Watermelon *(Shown on page 3)*
Sew a snap clip to the watermelon base. Work a Backstitch mouth, Satin Stitch eyes, and Straight Stitch "seeds" on watermelon. Layer and sew base and watermelon together.

Flower 1 *(Shown on page 4)*
Sew a snap clip to 1 flower base. On remaining flower base, work Straight Stitch "veins." Center and sew a mini flower and button to flower base. Layer and sew bases together.

Flower 2 *(Shown on page 3)*
Sew a snap clip to 1 flower base. If desired, embroider an initial on flower center. Sew flower center to remaining flower base with Running Stitches. Layer and sew bases together.

Flower 3 *(Shown top right)*
Sew a snap clip to 1 flower base. Sew flower center to remaining flower base with a Cross Stitch. Layer and sew bases together.

Acorn *(Shown below)*
Sew a snap clip to 1 acorn base. Layer cap on remaining acorn base and work Backstitch detail lines through both layers. Layer and sew bases together.

Pumpkin *(Shown on page 30)*
Sew a snap clip to 1 pumpkin base. On remaining pumpkin base, work Running Stitch "veins." Layer bases, insert stem between layers and sew bases together. Attach leaf with Backstitches.

Leaf *(Shown on page 30)*
Sew a snap clip to leaf base. Layer and sew base and small leaf together.

Cupcake *(Shown on page 31)*
Sew a snap clip to 1 cupcake base. Layer icing on remaining cupcake base then work a Backstitch mouth, Straight Stitch "sprinkles", and Satin Stitch eyes through both layers. Layer and sew bases together. Stitching through all layers, Backstitch detail lines on lower cupcake.

Turtle *(Shown on page 3)*
Sew a snap clip to the turtle base. Use Running Stitches to sew the shell to turtle base. Attach the flower with a Cross Stitch. Work Straight Stitch eyes and a Backstitch mouth.

Skull *(Shown on page 31)*
Sew a snap clip to 1 skull base. On remaining skull base, attach eyes with a Running Stitch, work a Satin Stitch nose, and a Blanket stitch mouth. Layer and sew bases together. Attach the flower with a Cross Stitch.

Tree *(Shown on page 31)*
Sew a snap clip to 1 round base. On remaining round base, center then attach tree with a Running Stitch. Layer and sew bases together.

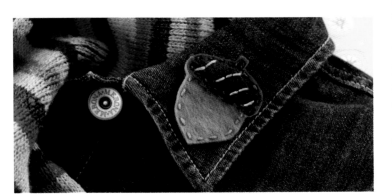

iPOD/MP3 PLAYER COZY

Let your creativity show while protecting your valuable electronics with this handy cozy. You can embellish your cozy with any design, pages 28-40, that reflects your unique personality. These cozies are so quick and easy to make, you might want to make some as gifts for all your music-loving friends.

Finished Size: 3" x 5"

Supplies
Supplies listed are for one cozy.
• Two 3" x 5" rectangles of felt
• Felt scraps
• Embroidery floss

*Please read **General Instructions**, pages 24-25, before beginning project. Follow **Using Patterns**, page 25, to adjust pattern size. Refer to **Embroidery Stitches**, page 26, for stitch techniques. Use 3 strands of floss for all stitching.*

1. Choose a design, pages 28-40, for the cozy front; size the pattern(s), if needed. Use pattern(s) to cut shape(s) from felt scraps.
2. Work Running Stitches across one short (top) edge of each rectangle.
3. Arrange, layer, and pin shape(s) to 1 rectangle. Sewing through all layers, use a Running Stitch to sew shape(s) to rectangle. Work embroidery details, if any, on shape(s).
4. Layer rectangles. Sewing through all layers, use a Running Stitch to sew rectangles together along 2 sides and across the bottom.

greeting CARD

> Miniature felt pennants, strung on lengths of embroidery floss, display a happy wish on a handcrafted greeting card. Birthday cards are always welcome gifts — even more so when they're lovingly handmade.

- Start with a purchased blank card and matching envelope.

- Choose your desired design(s) from the patterns, pages 28-40. We used the pennant, page 32.

- Follow **Using Patterns**, page 25, to adjust pattern size(s), if needed. Cut the shape(s) from felt.

- Use floss to embellish the shapes as desired, and to sew them to the front of the card.

- Stamp a sentiment on a scrap of coordinating card stock and glue to card.

Just a Thought
You can make cards for any occasion. Use the pumpkin and leaf patterns to make Thanksgiving cards. Sprinkle a Valentine's Day card with assorted-size hearts.

purse

We embellished our purse with a fun Funky Flower, but you can choose any design, pages 28-40, to decorate your purse.

Please read **General Instructions**, pages 24-25, before beginning project. **Note:** If using a different design, follow **Using Patterns**, page 25, to adjust pattern size(s), if needed. Refer to **Embroidery Stitches**, page 26, for stitch techniques. Use 6 strands of floss for all stitching unless otherwise noted.

Finished Size: approximately 13" x 13"

Supplies
Yardage is based on 72" wide felt.
- 1/2 yd of tan felt
- 9" x 12" rectangle of blue felt
- Embroidery floss - tan and blue
- Button - round 1" dia.
- Bamboo purse handles - round 6" dia.

1. Cut two 13" x 28" rectangles from cream felt.
2. Cut one of each Funky Flower petal 1-5, page 37, from blue felt.
3. Matching raw edges, layer cream rectangles; pin layers together.
4. Matching short edges, fold rectangles in half. The folded edge will be the bottom of the purse. Beginning 7" from top edges and going through all layers, Blanket Stitch side edges together (**Fig. 1**).
5. Turn purse wrong side out. Fold top edges of 1 side of the purse over 1 handle as shown in **Fig. 2**; pin.
6. Using 12 strands of floss, work 1/2" long Running Stitches spaced 1" apart (**Fig. 3**). Repeat for other handle. Turn purse right side out and remove all pins.
7. Working from largest to smallest, center and layer the Funky Flower petals; top petals with a button. Going through the button and all layers, sew the Funky Flower to one side of the purse, just below the handle.

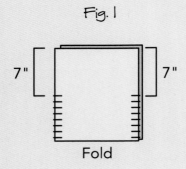

Fig. 1

7"   7"

Fold

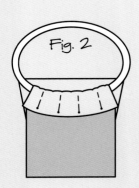

Fig. 2

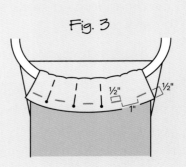

Fig. 3

1/2"   1/2"
1"

This "sew" simple purse is just right for holding all your necessities. It's so fast and easy that you might decide to make several!

hunny Bunny

This adorable felt bunny will delight any child. Make her as shown for a huggable stuffed animal. Reduce the pattern size and make a flat bunny to grace an Easter basket tag or hair clip. However you choose to use your Hunny Bunny, she is sure to bring smiles to all.

Finished Size: approximately 14" high (excluding ears)

Supplies
Yardage is based on 36" wide felt.
- ½ yd of tan felt
- 9" x 12" rectangle of light pink felt
- 9" x 12" rectangle of medium pink felt
- Embroidery floss - tan, pink, green, and brown
- Polyester fiberfill

*Please read **General Instructions**, pages 24-25, before beginning project. Follow **Using Patterns**, page 25, to adjust pattern size. Refer to **Embroidery Stitches**, page 26, for stitch techniques. Use 3 strands of floss for all stitching.*

Cutting
1. For a 14" high bunny, enlarge the patterns, pages 34-35, to 143%.
2. Cut two 2 bodies and 4 outer ears from tan felt.
3. Cut 2 inner ears from medium pink felt.
4. Cut 1 collar, 3 flower centers, and 2 dresses from light pink felt.
5. Cut 4 flowers from green felt.

Assembling
Bunny
1. Center 1 inner ear on 1 outer ear; pin. Sew around inner ear using Running Stitches; layer and pin to a second outer ear. Whipstitch edges of outer ears together. Repeat with remaining inner and outer ears to make 2 ears.
2. On 1 body, stitch a face by working a Backstitch mouth and Satin Stitch eyes and nose. Add Straight Stitch whiskers.
3. Layer bodies; pin. Folding straight ends of ears to make a pleat, insert and pin ears between layers where indicated on pattern. Leave top of head open and use a Running Stitch to sew across ears and a Whipstitch to sew the remainder of the layers together.
4. Stuff firmly with fiberfill. **Tip:** Use a knitting needle, chopstick or skewer to help push fiberfill down into arms and legs.

5. Whipstitch opening in head closed.
6. Layer 2 flowers; sew around edges with a Running Stitch. Center 1 flower center on flower; pin. Stitching through all layers, sew flower to the base of 1 ear with a Cross Stitch.

Dress
1. To make dress front, arrange 2 flowers and 2 flower centers on 1 dress. Stitching through all layers, work a Cross Stitch in the center of each flower center.
2. Layer dress front, bunny and remaining dress. Matching raw edges, Whipstitch dress together at shoulder seams.
3. Matching straight raw edges, Whipstitch each side of dress from underarm to hem. Whipstitch around bottom edge of dress.
4. With opening at center back, place collar around neck. Overlapping as needed, adjust collar to fit snuggly around your bunny's neck; pin. Use Running Stitches to sew flat edge of collar to neck and scalloped edge of collar to dress. Work a Cross Stitch on each scallop.

coffee cup
cozy

Keep your coffee hot with a handy Coffee Cup Cozy. We chose a flower to brighten our cozy, but you can embellish your cozy with any design from pages 28-40.

Finished Cozy Size: approximately 12" x 4"

Supplies
- Two 9" x 12" rectangles of felt (we used blue)
- One 9" x 12" rectangle of felt (we used red)
- Embroidery floss (we used red)
- Button
- Elastic ponytail holder

*Please read **General Instructions**, pages 24-25, before beginning project. Follow **Using Patterns**, page 25, to adjust pattern size. Use 2 strands of floss for all stitching.*

1. Measure the height and circumference of your cup. Allowing for a 1"-2" overlap when buttoned, size patterns, page 36. **Note:** To fit our cup, 6" high with a 9" circumference, we enlarged the patterns to 114%.
2. Cut 2 large cozies and 1 flower from blue felt. Cut 1 small cozy and 1 flower center from red felt.
3. Matching raw edges, layer large cozies. Insert one end of ponytail holder between layers on straight end of cozy; pin.
4. Center and layer the flower and flower center on the small cozy; pin. Stitching through all layers, use a Running Stitch, page 27, to sew the flower and flower center to the cozy.
5. Center small cozy on large cozy; pin. Stitching through all layers and securely catching end of ponytail holder in stitching, sew cozies together using a Running Stitch.
6. Wrap cozy around your cup to mark button placement. Sew button to cozy.

TOTE BAG

From groceries to workout clothes to craft projects, it seems that we always need to carry items that are too large for the average purse. Purchased tote bags can be functional, but not necessarily attractive. Now you can up the cute factor of any ready-made tote by adding a fun felt appliqué!

Simply browse though the patterns, pages 28-40, for the perfect design, (we chose the flower, page 30) then follow **Using Patterns**, page 25, to adjust the size, if needed. Cut the shape(s) from felt and embellish as desired (we embroidered an initial in the center). Stitch your shape(s) to your tote using embroidery floss and a Running Stitch, page 27.

Cute factor: 10!

Just A Thought
For a touch of bling, add buttons, beads, or rhinestones to your appliqué.

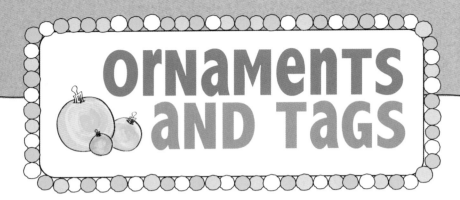

Ornaments and Tags

These festive ornaments and tags are quick and easy to make, and they're a fun family project on a snowy day. We chose holiday-themed designs for our ornaments, but you can use any of the designs on pages 28-40. Why not make several for teachers' gifts or gift exchanges? The tag, page 16, is simply an ornament with a piece of cardstock sewn to the back — how easy is that?

Finished Approximate Heights:
tree - 2½", dove - 3", star - 3", gingerbread house - 3¼"

Supplies
- Felt scraps
- Embroidery floss
- ⅛" wide ribbon
- Cardstock (for tags only)

Assembling
*Please read **General Instructions**, pages 24-25, before beginning project. Follow **Using Patterns**, page 25, to adjust pattern size(s), if desired. Refer to **Embroidery Stitches**, page 26, for stitch techniques. Use 2 strands of floss for all stitching unless otherwise noted.*

Tree
1. Cut 2 round bases and 1 tree, page 31, from felt scraps.

2. For front, center tree on 1 base; pin. Sew around tree using a Running Stitch.

3. Layer front and remaining base; pin. Fold an 8" length of ribbon in half and insert raw ends between layers at top of tree. Use a Running Stitch to sew layers together, catching ribbon ends in stitching.

Star
1. Cut 1 small and 2 large stars, page 38, from felt scraps.

2. For front, use 1 strand of floss and a Backstitch to freehand embroider the word Joy on small star. Center, layer, and pin small star on 1 large star. Sew around small star using a Running Stitch.

3. Layer front and remaining star; pin. Fold a 8" length of ribbon in half and insert raw ends between layers at top of star point. Use a Running Stitch to sew layers together, catching ribbon ends in stitching.

Dove

1. Cut 2 doves and 1 wing, page 38, from felt scraps.

2. For front, layer and pin wing on 1 dove. Work Running Stitches to attach wing. Work a Smyrna Cross Stitch eye.

3. Layer front and remaining dove; pin. Fold an 8" length of ribbon in half and insert raw ends between layers at center of dove's back. Use a Running Stitch to sew layers together, catching ribbon ends in stitching.

Gingerbread House

1. Cut 2 houses, 1 door, and 1 roof, page 38, from felt scraps.

2. For front, layer and pin door and roof on 1 house. Work Running Stitches around door and roof. Work a French Knot doorknob. Using 6 strands of floss, work Straight Stitch windows.

3. Layer front and remaining house; pin. Fold an 8" length of ribbon in half and insert raw ends between layers at top of house. Use a Running Stitch to sew layers together, catching ribbon ends in stitching.

Instructions continued on page 16.

Instructions continued from page 15.

Tags

1. To make a tag from any of the ornament patterns, follow Step 1 of selected ornament instructions to cut shapes from felt, then use the pattern to cut 1 of the same shape from cardstock. Trim the cardstock shape slightly smaller than the felt shapes.

2. If desired, use markers to write a message on the cardstock shape.

3. Follow Step 2 of ornament instructions.

4. Layer front, remaining shape, and cardstock shape. Fold an 8" length of ribbon in half and insert folded end between felt layers of shape. Use a Running Stitch to sew layers together, catching folded end of ribbon in stitching.

Just a Thought

Tags aren't just for Christmas! Wouldn't the turtle or cupcake make a cute tag for a birthday present? You could craft a bunny tag for an Easter Basket or whip up a one-of-a-kind heart tag for a box of Valentine's Day candy!

hair clip HOLDER

Every little (or big) girl needs a handy place to corral her hair clips, bows, and barrettes. This super fast, super easy Hair Clip Holder is the perfect answer to organizing those hair accessories!

Finished Size: approximately 33" long

Supplies
- Felt scraps (we used pink and brown)
- Fabric scrap (we used brown print)
- 24" length of $^{7}/_{8}$" wide ribbon
- 10" length of $^{3}/_{8}$" wide ribbon
- Button (we used an $^{11}/_{16}$" dia.)
- Embroidery floss (we used pink and brown)

You can use any design, pages 28-40, to embellish your Clip Holder (we chose the flower, page 33, and enlarged the patterns to 200%).

*Please read **General Instructions**, pages 24-25, before beginning project. Follow **Using Patterns**, page 25, to adjust pattern size(s). Refer to **Embroidery Stitches**, page 26, for stitch techniques. Use 6 strands of floss for all stitching.*

1. Cut 2 flowers (ours are 4" dia.) and 2 circles (ours are 1$^{1}/_{2}$" dia.) from felt scraps. Cut 1 flower center (ours is 2" dia.) from fabric.
2. For front, center and sew flower center to 1 flower using a Running Stitch. Work long Straight Stitches to make flower details.
3. Layer front and remaining flower. Fold narrow ribbon in half and insert raw ends between layers; pin. Insert one raw end of wide ribbon between layers, opposite narrow ribbon; pin. Catching ribbon ends in stitching, sew layers together with a Running Stitch.
4. Layer circles. Insert remaining raw end of wide ribbon between layers; pin. Catching ribbon end in stitching, sew layers together with a Running Stitch. Sew the button to the center of the circle.

project envelope & needlebook

In airports, doctor's offices — we spend so much of our time just waiting! How often have you thought, "I wish I had a project to work on?" This clever felt envelope is just the right size to hold the coordinating needlebook, a pair of embroidery scissors, floss, and a small project. And it slips easily into a purse or tote bag so you never have to be without again!

Just a Thought
The envelope also works great for holding make-up, pens and pencils, or even coupons — the possibilities are endless!

Envelope
Finished Size: 8" x 4"

Follow **Fig. 1** to fold and pin the lower third of an 8" x 12" felt rectangle up to form a pocket. Using 6 strands of floss, work Running Stitches, page 27, around 3 sides, securing pocket. Center and sew a button to the pocket front (**Fig. 2**).

For the flap, fold the top third of the rectangle down over the pocket. Mark buttonhole placement and then cut a slit in the flap to make a buttonhole.

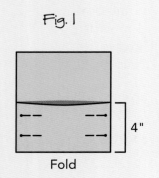

Fig. 1

4"

Fold

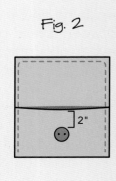

Fig. 2

2"

Needlebook
Finished Size: closed 2¹/₂" x 3¹/₂"

From coordinating felt scraps, cut 1 outer book 5" x 3¹/₂", 1 inner book 4¹/₂" x 3", and 1 pocket 2" x 3". Center and layer the inner and outer books; pin. Matching short ends, fold the book in half. Using a Running Stitch, page 27, and stitching through all layers, sew ¹/₈" from fold.

Using your choice of patterns, pages 28-40, and following **Using Patterns**, page 25, to adjust pattern size, embellish the front of the needlebook as desired.

Using a Running Stitch, sew along 1 long edge of the small pocket. With stitched edge to the right, center pocket on inside front cover of needlebook. Stitching through all layers, use a Running Stitch to sew remaining 3 sides to cover.

GARLANDS

Add a little fun to an ordinary day or special occasion when you whip up one of these oh-so-easy garlands. We used the hearts, page 37, and the circles, page 39, but you can use any of the designs found on pages 28-40 for your garland. Make your garland any length you desire by adding felt shapes until you achieve your desired length. Garlands shown range from 66"-72" long. The Woodland Garland, page 22, was made using a variety of outdoor-themed patterns.

HEART GARLAND

Finished Approximate Heights:
large heart - 3¹/₂"
small heart - 2¹/₂"

Supplies
Supplies listed are for one garland.
• Five 9" x 12" rectangles of felt
  (we used 2 red, 2 light pink, and
  1 hot pink)
• Embroidery floss

*Please read **General Instructions**, pages 24-25, before beginning project. Follow **Using Patterns**, page 25, to adjust pattern size(s), if desired. Use 6 strands of floss for all stitching.*

1. Cut desired number of large and small hearts, page 37, from felt (we used 24 of each size).

2. Mixing colors as desired, center and layer 1 small heart on each large heart; pin.

3. Cut a 36" length of floss; knot one end. Starting at the point, work a Running Stitch, page 27, through the center of 1 layered heart.

4. Keeping the orientation of the hearts the same, sew through the center of the second heart. Continue adding layered hearts in the same manner.

5. When you run out of floss, finish with a knot on the wrong side of a heart. Begin at stopping point with a new length of floss and continue sewing until all layered hearts are connected.

CHRISTMAS GARLAND

Using patterns, page 39, cut assorted size circles from light green, green, and red felt (we used 24 circles). Randomly mixing sizes and colors, follow Steps 3 - 5 of Heart Garland, until all circles are connected and garland is the desired length.

For a slightly different look, try layering circles, like the Heart Garland, page 20.

Just a Thought
Welcome spring with a garland of flowers or fall with a garland of pumpkins and leaves. Patterns for these shapes are found on page 30.

WOODLAND GARLAND

Instructions given are for making one shape from each design. Make your garland unique by making as many shapes of each design as desired. You might even want to include other designs in your garland — like the turtle on page 30!

Finished Approximate Heights:
owl - 4^1/$_4$", mushroom - 3^1/$_2$", hedgehog - 3^1/$_4$", tree - 5^1/$_2$", redbird - 2^1/$_2$"

Supplies
- Felt scraps (we used red, dark red, tan, brown, green, blue, white, pink, and gold)
- Embroidery floss (we used red, tan, dark brown, green, blue, and gold)
- Polyester fiberfill
- ^{1}/$_8$ yd of cream fabric
- Jute or twine

Assembling the Shapes
Please read **General Instructions**, pages 24-25, before beginning project. Follow **Using Patterns**, page 25, to adjust pattern size(s). Refer to **Embroidery Stitches**, page 26, for stitch techniques.

Ties
1. For each shape in your garland, cut one 1" x 5" tie from cream fabric. Matching short ends, fold tie in half; press. Set ties aside.

Owl
Use 2 strands of floss for all stitching unless otherwise indicated.
1. Cut 2 owl bases, 1 eye, and 1 beak, page 28, from felt scraps.
2. To make front, layer and pin eyes and beak on 1 base. Work 3 Straight Stitches to attach beak. Work Satin Stitch pupils. Work Backstitch "feathers".
3. Layer front and remaining base; pin. Leaving top of head open between the ears, use 6 strands of floss and a Running Stitch to sew front and back together. Fill owl with fiberfill. Insert folded end of 1 tie in opening on head. Close opening with Running Stitches, catching tie in stitching.

Mushroom
Use 3 strands of floss for all stitching.
1. Cut 3 dots, 2 caps, and 2 stems, page 40, from felt scraps.
2. Straight Stitch dots to 1 cap. Layer cap on 1 stem; pin. Use a Running Stitch to sew bottom edge of cap to stem. Repeat for remaining cap and stem.
3. Matching wrong sides, layer mushrooms; pin. Leaving an opening across top of cap, use a Running Stitch to sew layers together.
4. Fill mushroom with fiberfill. Insert folded end of 1 tie in opening. Close opening with Running Stitches, catching tie in stitching.

Hedgehog
Use 3 strands of floss for all stitching.
1. Cut 2 hedgehog bases, 1 fur, 1 nose, and 1 flower, page 28, from felt scraps.
2. To make front, Straight Stitch nose to 1 base and work a Satin Stitch eye.
3. Layer fur, front, and remaining base; pin. Use a Running Stitch to sew layers together around legs and nose and to sew fur to front around face only. `
4. Leaving an opening across the top, use a Running Stitch to sew all layers together around fur.
5. Fill hedgehog with fiberfill. Insert folded end of 1 tie in opening. Close opening with Running Stitches, catching tie in stitching. Attach flower with a Cross Stitch.

Tree

Use 3 strands of floss for all stitching.

1. Cut 2 treetops and 2 trunks, page 40, from felt scraps.
2. Position 1 trunk on 1 treetop; pin. Repeat for remaining trunk and treetop, in reverse. Check to be sure trunks and treetops align when layered.
3. Use a Running Stitch to sew around branches to attach trunk to treetop. Repeat for remaining trunk and treetop.
4. Layer trees; pin. Beginning at bottom edge of treetop, sew trunks together.
5. Leaving an opening across top of treetop, sew treetops together.
6. Fill tree with fiberfill. Insert folded end of 1 tie in opening. Close opening with Running Stitches, catching tie in stitching.

Redbird

Use 6 strands of floss for all stitching.

1. Cut 2 bird bases and 1 wing, page 28, from felt scraps.
2. To make front, layer and pin wing on 1 base. Work Running Stitches to attach wing. Work a Cross Stitch eye.
3. Layer front and remaining base; pin. Leaving an opening between head and tail, use a Running Stitch to sew layers together. Fill redbird with fiberfill. Insert folded end of 1 tie in opening. Close opening with Running Stitches, catching tie in stitching.

Assembling the Garland

1. Cute jute or twine the desired finished length.
2. Arranging as desired, tie each shape onto the jute.

GENERAL INSTRUCTIONS

To make your crafting easier and more enjoyable, we encourage you to carefully read all of the general instructions and familiarize yourself with the individual project instructions before you get started.

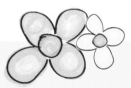

Supplies
Supplies listed below are needed for all projects. Individual project instructions include supplies specific to that project.

FELT
Projects were made using wool felt or eco-felt. Eco-felt is made using Eco-fil™, a polyester fiber created from 100% post-consumer recycled plastic bottles. Both wool felt and eco-felt are available in approximately 9" x 12" sheets or by the yard in 36", 60", or 72" widths.

THREAD
Projects were stitched using six-strand cotton embroidery floss. Individual project instructions specify the number of strands to use.

NEEDLES
A sharp point is necessary to pierce felt, but the size and type of needle is an individual choice. The eye needs to be large enough to accommodate the number of strands of floss you will be using but small enough to pass through the holes in buttons (if used).

Embroidery needles, sometimes referred to as crewel needles, usually work well. Sizes range from #3 - #10 and they are available in individual and multi-size packages. Keep in mind that the lower the number, the larger the needle.

SCISSORS
Use fabric scissors to cut out felt shapes and utility scissors for cutting paper patterns. Small sharp embroidery scissors are handy for clipping thread and trimming "fuzzies" from the edges of finished shapes.

USING PATTERNS

The patterns in this book can be reduced or enlarged to any size, allowing you to use any design for any project. Enlarge a pattern and use it to make a stuffed shape (like the mushroom in Woodland Garland, shown on page 23) or reduce the same pattern to make a tiny embellishment (like the mushroom on the Mini Hair Clip, shown on page 3). Many of the patterns, as printed, work well for a medium-size hair clip or embellishment on a coffee cup cozy.

If a pattern is printed at the desired finished size, either trace the pattern onto tracing paper or make a photocopy of the pattern; cut out pattern on outer black line.

Sizing Patterns

To change the size of a pattern, divide the desired height of the pattern by the actual height of the pattern. Multiply the result by 100 and photocopy the pattern at this percentage.

For example, you want to enlarge the pattern to be $3^1/2$" high and the pattern as printed is 2" high.

    $3^1/2 \div 2 = 1.75$
    $1.75 \times 100 = 175\%$
    Copy the pattern at 175%

Or, to make the pattern smaller, say $1^1/2$" high, use the same formula.

    $1^1/2 \div 2 = .75$
    $.75 \times 100 = 75\%$
    Copy the pattern at 75%

If a design has multiple pieces, remember to size all pattern pieces at the same percentage. Cut out pattern(s) on outer black line.

WORKING WITH FELT

Place patterns, printed or traced side up, on felt; pin. Cut out shapes even with edges of pattern. Repeat for each pattern piece needed for your project.

Felt does not have a right or wrong side. If a felt shape is embroidered or embellished, the decorated side becomes the right side. When instructed to layer shapes, place an embellished shape right side up on top of an undecorated shape. For shapes that are not decorated, such as the Heart Garland, page 20, simply layer the shapes.

FINISHING

*Shapes can be finished flat like the hair clips shown on page 3, or dimensionally like the Woodland Garland shapes shown on page 23. The instructions below are **general** guidelines for finishing. Refer to individual project instructions for more details.*

- Cut 2 of each base shape and 1 of each embellishment shape.

- When stitching, always begin and end on the back side of a single shape or between the pieces of layered shapes to hide knots.

- Sew snap clips or pinbacks (if used) to undecorated side of base shape.

- Most of the projects were made using 6 strands of floss to sew layered shapes together. For smaller projects, you may want to use 3 strands.

- For flat finishing, sew layered shapes together with a Running Stitch.

- For dimensional finishing, sew layers together with a Running Stitch, leaving an opening near the top of the shape. Fill with polyester fiberfill, insert hanger (if used) and close opening with Running Stitches. **Note:** Hunny Bunny, shown on page 11, is sewn together using a Whipstitch instead of a Running Stitch.

embroidery STITCHES

Backstitch

Come up at 1, go down at 2, and come up at 3 (**Fig. 1**). Length of stitches may be varied as desired.

Fig. 1

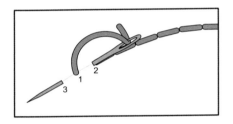

Blanket Stitch

Come up at 1, go down at 2, and come up at 3, keeping thread below point of needle (**Fig. 2**).

Fig. 2

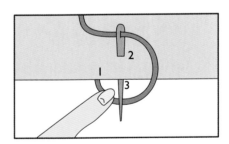

Cross Stitch

Come up at 1 and go down at 2. Come up at 3 and go down at 4 (**Fig. 3**).

Fig. 3

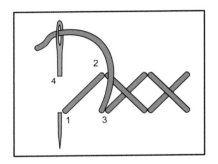

French Knot

Follow **Figs. 4 – 5** to complete French Knots. Come up at 1. Wrap thread once around needle and insert needle at 2, holding end of thread with non-stitching fingers. Tighten knot, then pull needle through, holding floss until it must be released.

Fig. 4

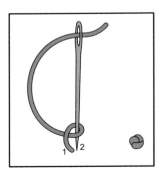

Fig. 5

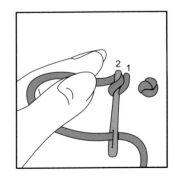

Cupcake Icing

Cupcake Base

Acorn Base

Cap

Skull Flower

Skull Eye

Skull Base

Round Base

Tree

31

Watermelon Base

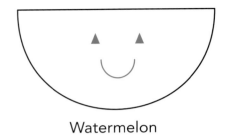

Watermelon

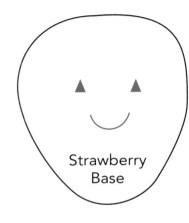

Strawberry Base

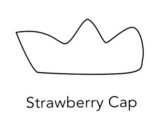

Strawberry Cap

Oval Base

Candy Corn Middle

Candy Corn Top

Candy Corn Bottom

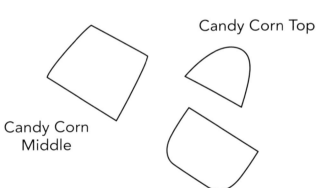

Pennant

Fleur de Lis

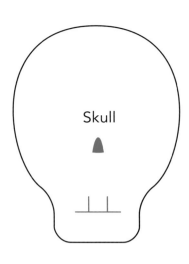

Skull

Skull Eye
Cut 2

Flower Stem

Flower Circles

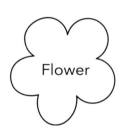

Flower

Skull Flower

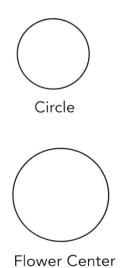

Circle

Flower Center

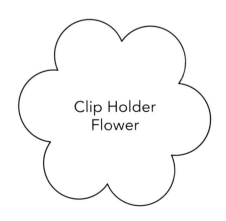

Clip Holder Flower

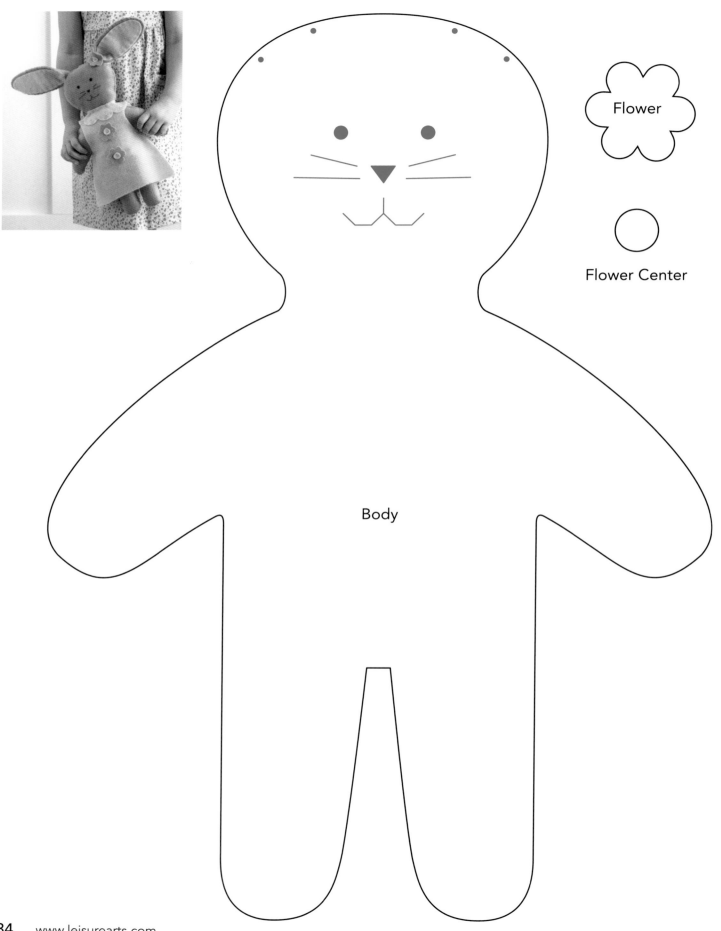

Flower

Flower Center

Body

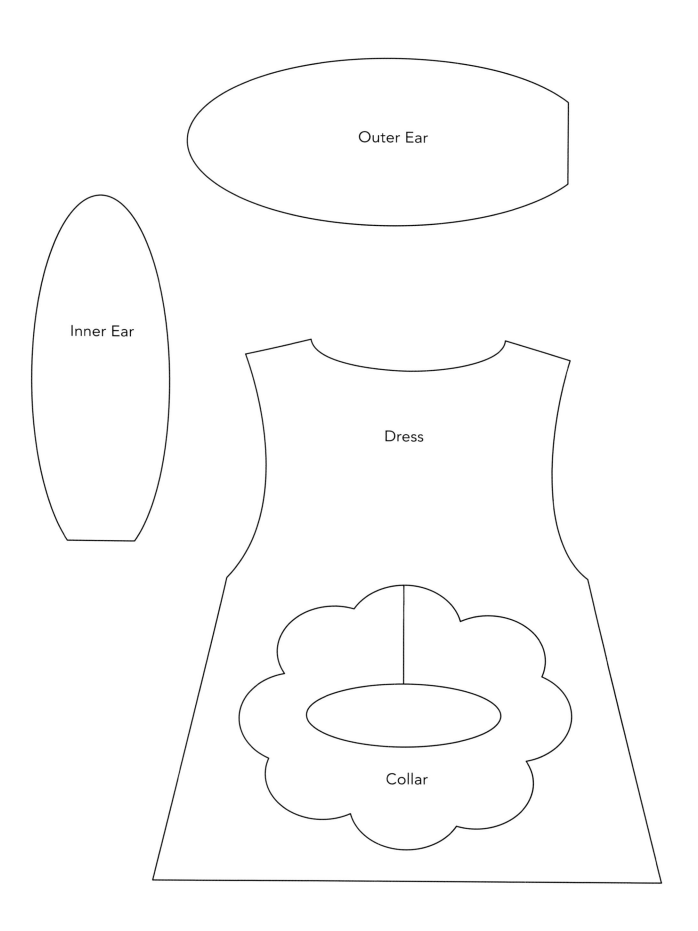

Outer Ear

Inner Ear

Dress

Collar

Large Cozy

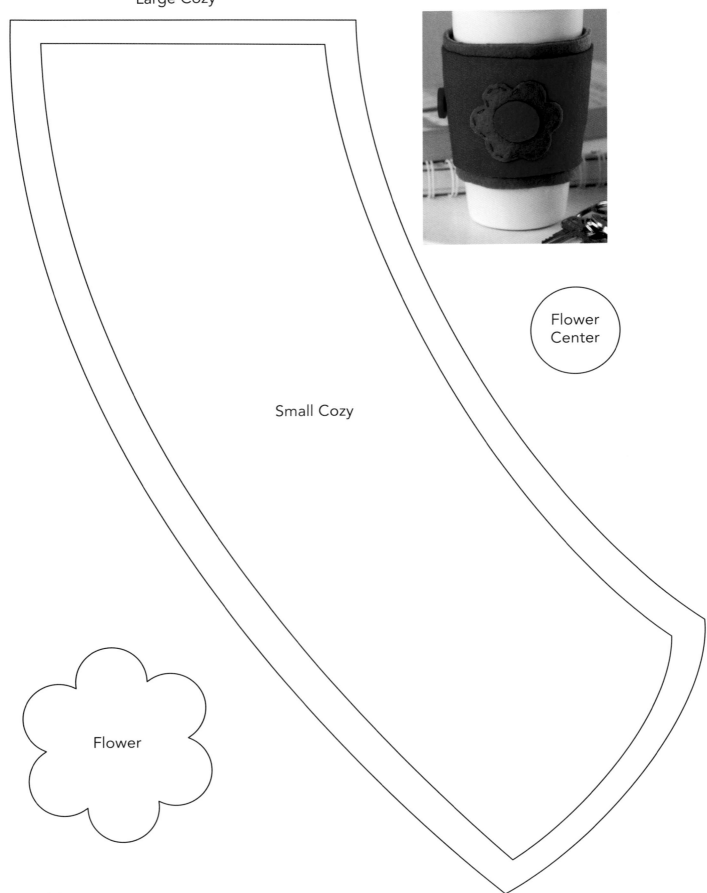

Small Cozy

Flower Center

Flower

Large Heart

Small Heart

Funky
Flower
Petal 5

Funky Flower Petal 4

Funky Flower Petal 3

Funky Flower Petal 2

Funky Flower Petal 1

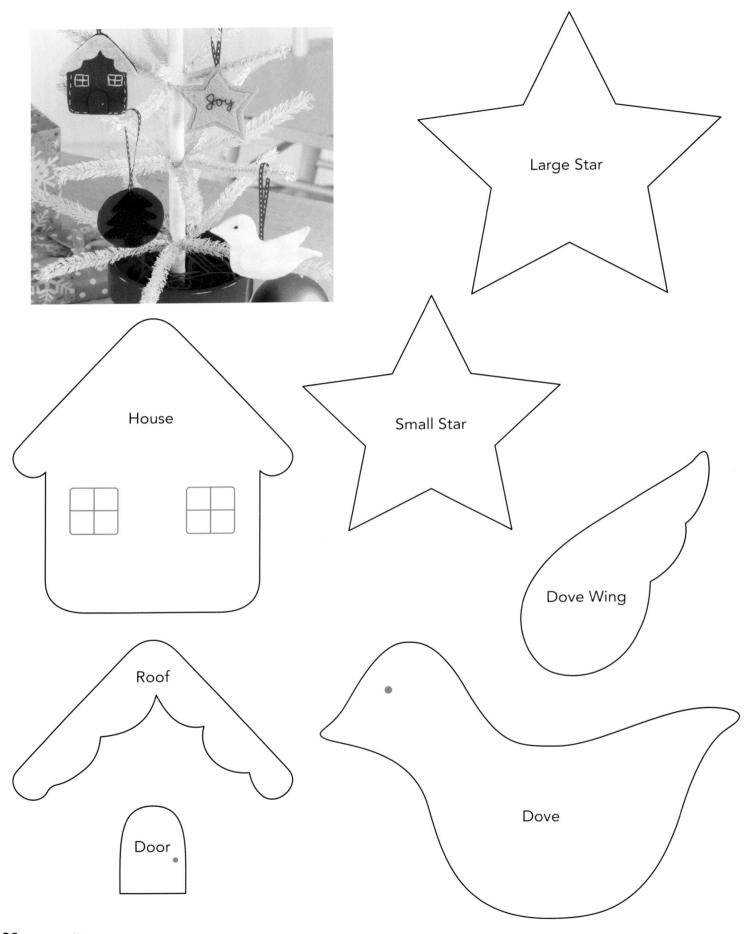

Large Star

House

Small Star

Dove Wing

Roof

Dove

Door

Christmas Garland
Medium Circle

Christmas Garland
Extra-Small Circle

Christmas Garland
Large Circle

Christmas Garland
Small Circle

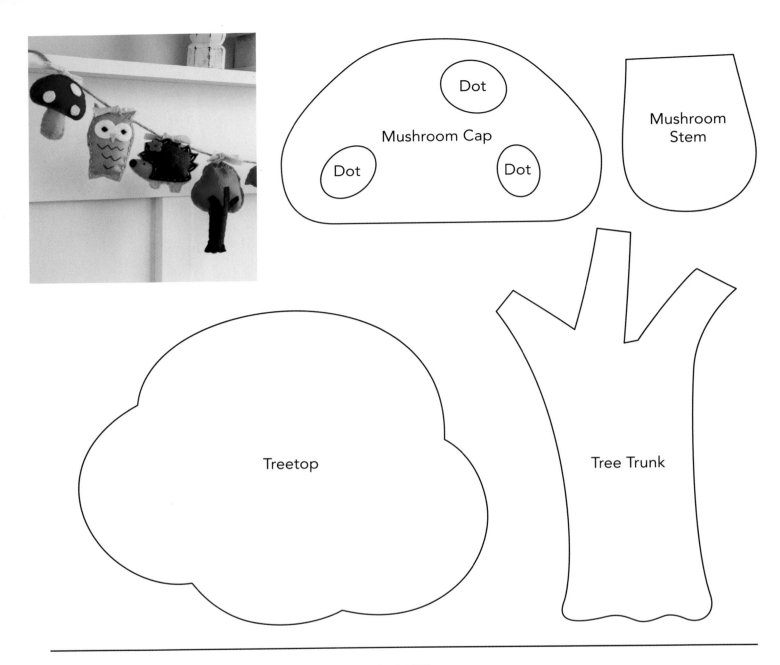

Mushroom Cap

Dot

Dot

Dot

Mushroom Stem

Treetop

Tree Trunk

CREDITS

Technical Editor – Lisa Lancaster; Instructional Writer – Jean Lewis; Editorial Writer – Susan McManus Johnson;
Senior Graphic Artist – Lora Puls; Graphic Artist – Kara Darling; Photography Stylist – Sondra Daniel ; Photographer – Ken West